Marketing for Rookies

How to Go From

Marketing Rookie to Rockstar

Hillary Dow

To Robin and Bob Konieczko, my mom and dad. Thank you for teaching me how to fill my world with love, set a goal and see it through, and live a life of adventure.

Contents

Foreword

When you know you have a book inside you, and you know you want to help others, an amazing opportunity lies before you. You simply need to find the courage to venture down an unfamiliar path.

I began my journey as an author on July 11, 2018. I know the precise date because I have it written on the back of a Mac's Grill business card that is now tucked in a box of ticket stubs and other precious memorabilia. My husband, Adam, and I have a standing weekly lunch date. We both get away from work, the kids are off enjoying their own daily routines, and he and I enjoy an hour all to ourselves. Some weeks we're dining al fresco and always patronizing one of the local businesses nearby.

Chatter during our "date lunches," as I fondly call them, may consist of funny stories recalling the wacky things our children Tyler and Eva did or said, planning trips and adventures, or talking about our work and the future. We talk about what drives us, what energizes us, our goals and aspirations, and we encourage one another.

On that particular day in mid-July I looked over my Mediterranean salad at Adam, and I said, "You should write a book. You would be an exceptional author." As I paused and watched for his reaction, I saw the gears begin to turn. I love it when you can visibly tell that someone has just kicked their mind and imagination into high gear. That is what I saw.

I then asked, "What would you write about?" As he continued munching on his own Mediterranean salad, he chewed on that question for a bit. It wasn't long before he had an idea for the topic of his first book. A couple years back, an Appalachian Trail thru-hiker named Geraldine Largay wandered off the trail near the Bigelow range in the western mountains of Maine. Tragically, she was not found during the days and weeks following her disappearance. She died, lost in the Maine woods.

A lifelong hiker and avid outdoorsman, Adam has hiked in that region in the past, and I grew up in that area (we now live 75 miles south of there) and still have many family members there. I know several of the amazing men and women who aided in the search. As heartbreaking as the story is, it was what immediately came to mind when he pondered the notion of writing a book.

Nearing the end of his salad, Adam asked me, "And what about you? What would you write about?"

Without skipping a beat, I immediately and effortlessly replied: "I would write a book about marketing because I want to help others be successful. There are many marketers within professional service businesses who could take their skills to new heights, with support and coaching." With 20 years of lessons learned, I wanted to share my views and knowledge with like-minded professionals.

Over the years I've had many public speaking opportunities, where I shared insights and experiences about marketing. I feel an indescribable sense of purpose when I share what I know and I see people sit up a little straighter, lean in as they listen, or widen their eyes and lift their eyebrows when I share a key point or reach an exciting conclusion. When I know, deep in my heart, that I'm sparking thought and curiosity in someone's mind and that I'm making a positive difference in how someone thinks and what they aspire to be—that, my friends, is what purpose looks like for me.

So began a six-month journey of waking up at 4:00 am, six days a week, and slicing in time on weekends to turn our date-lunch conversation into reality. I want to thank Adam for being an inspiration, my best friend and partner in this amazing life adventure, and the most amazing father imaginable to our two children.

Lastly, thank you, my reader, for being a part of this journey. My hope for you is that you too will find inspiration and purpose in the work you do. Sit up a little straighter, lean in a bit more often, and celebrate your achievements.

1

Own Your Path

This book is written for you, with a twist. We have many choices throughout the course of our lives, many with significant impact and influence over our entire story. When it comes to our choices regarding friends, education, how to invest our money, what we do in our down time, what we eat, how we exercise, the work we do, the profession we choose, our life partner, family, every decision lays a stone and defines our path.

As you read this book, I ask that you remind yourself that it is OK—no, not just OK, but imperative—to put yourself first. The only way to be present and fully engaged in your life is to take care of yourself first.

As we move along, we lay many stones along the path of life. Sometimes they get knocked out of sight, get squished down into the mud, or create tripping obstacles you'll move heaven and earth to avoid. Some stones shine up at you with happy little flecks of mica, some are worn smooth from going through the paces, and others are utterly and wonderfully raw, rough, and jagged. Sure, this is a metaphor for your life's journey, but it's a valid one. Your path is unique to you. When you put yourself first, you're forced to make choices. Sometimes choices position you to seize an amazing opportunity. Others help you maneuver curveballs, achieve milestones, or celebrate when you overcome a difficult and rewarding challenge. Another valuable choice is to simply relax and be centered in mindful rest and rejuvenation.

Know that your path is your own. Take responsibility for it. Own it. Life can be messy and painful, but it is also exhilarating and profound. You're reading this book for a reason. Do you view your life as the most amazing and exciting puzzle in the world? Do you look ahead and dream, plan, and take action? Or are you constantly looking behind at what has been? Do you settle with circumstances, or do you change circumstances? Are there experiences along your path that you are proud of, or a lot of missed opportunities?

Intentional Mindset

One constant you can count on is that you will always have a ridiculous amount to manage in all areas of your life. So be intentional about what you do, including the work you choose.

So what's the twist? The reasons fueling the intent behind our choices—they're the twist. Your path is your own, but it will continuously converge with countless people, purposes, projects, life lessons, curveballs, and so on. At times you'll be surrounded by support, and other times the pressure will seem unbearable. The secret to maintaining life balance is being intentional and true to ourselves, while approaching life, people, and our work with intent, kindness, and conviction.

I contend that the ingredients we use to kick up the flavor of our professional path make the difference between a plain, simple bowl of warm oatmeal and a bowl of steel-cut oats with toasted almonds, fresh blueberries, and vanilla yogurt and a drizzle of coconut oil on top—blueberry blast! Stock your cupboard with knockout ingredients and you're a lot more likely to make knockout food. Intentionally fill or even sprinkle your day with influences and value from various corners of your life, and you will create variety and enrichment. If you are always holding yourself back, if new and fun ingredients never venture their way into your kitchen, you may never know how incredibly awesome blueberry blast is. By adding this book to your library, you've added an awesome ingredient to your proverbial kitchen. Just think of all the amazing "meals" you're going to cook up!

Variety and experimentation are essential, but they are also often very daunting. Through trial and error we learn what will be successful, what will be effective, and what will fail or fall flat. If we're paying attention—and we should be—we learn, react, and veer away from things that are ineffective and replace them with new strategies and tactics. Take the bowl of steel-cut oats: If you don't invest additional time and preparation to transform them, you're bound to keep eating plain, run-of-the-mill oats.

Putting Yourself First

Take a moment and think back to a time when you felt content in your life. Your close relationships were meaningful and brought joy to your life. You were enrolled in or recently completed a training series or course work. You were adding new skills to your arsenal. You were receiving praise for your contributions at work. You felt physically fit and comfortable in your own skin. Your imagination and creativity were engaged and influencing your thinking.

Perhaps you're recalling several points along your path when all or some of these statements were true. Now ask yourself, "Was I putting myself first at that point? Were my actions influencing and impacting others?"

An essential place to remember to put yourself first is at work. People working as a team, always in support of one another and the business, is how businesses and organizations succeed. But that requires putting yourself first and being a team player; mastering both will lead to success. People and specialties are intertwined and interdependent of one another. For example, a dentist has a whole lot of downtime if patients aren't scheduled properly. When a major advertising promotion falls flat, the planned bump in patient appointments doesn't materialize, slowing the pipeline of scheduled appointments for the new hygienist. Or the patient having an annual cleaning misses the dentist's exam because the dentist is in the middle of a procedure. When the number of scheduled appointments is up and insurance claims are submitted in a timely manner, revenue projections stay on target and in line to meet year-end budget goals. The web of multidiscipline processes is applicable in every business. Every web simply has a different design.

Putting ourselves first but working in support of others is not counterintuitive. On the contrary, staying focused on your responsibilities and your own development drives you to achieve goals over time. When you remain focused on how your work contributes to the whole, you methodically and consistently make forward progress, for you and for the business.

Have you ever had a project that required you to utilize a software application that you were familiar with but in no way an expert at? As you got into the project, you may have found yourself muddling through the software as best you could, knowing that there had to be better ways of organizing and executing the tasks at hand. In the back of your mind you found yourself saying, if only I knew how to do X, I am certain my time would be spent more efficiently, and the final output for the project would be better. Or, if only I had X software so I could execute routine tasks more easily. In that moment, did you pause and recognize that you needed something to do your work to the best of your ability? Did you speak up on your own behalf?

Taking the time to continuously develop your skills and gain access to the tools necessary to do your work is critically important to ensure you are working at your highest possible contribution. With your focus set on efficiency and completing the most valuable work, you put yourself in a position to help the business and, just as importantly, yourself succeed.

When I first began working in the professional services sector, I was my own advocate. And I was vocal. I asked to take on new and different responsibilities, to have new software installed on my workstation, and to attend training seminars and webinars. I managed my time to allow for new tasks and responsibilities. By asking for more and by focusing on developing skills in areas that truly interested me, I worked my way out of an administrative assistant position and invented a new position in the business, marketing director, a position that still exists there today.

Because I continuously invested in my own growth and development, the business owner invested in me as well. The effort I put in was returned in new clients, stickier relationships with existing clients, and development of an awesome corporate culture. With these three stakeholder groups in mind—new clients, existing clients, and internal clients—your focus on self will pay off in a number of ways. The key is to stay focused and committed to the work that offers the most valuable return.

You may be reading this book and saying to yourself, I want that. I want to work my way out of the 20 other daily responsibilities on my plate and focus my efforts entirely on marketing and business development. You may be finding yourself thinking lately, "Boy, don't I absolutely love working with the media, managing social media for the business, and working a room at a networking event. My drive comes from bringing in a new client or from expanding the scope of an existing client. What an accomplishment. This is what I really love doing." If that's the case, listen to that little voice in the back of your mind.

Put yourself first. Plot a course that defines your own path and go for it!

Rookie Tips. Throughout this book you'll see a number of Rookie Tips. These get directly to the heart of lessons I've learned over the years, lessons that may serve you well while saving time and frustration. It's wise to learn from the trial and error of others. Been there, done that! I'd love for you to excel in similar circumstances, such as listening to that little voice in the back of your mind. You've got one life. The sooner you begin to follow your own north star, the sooner you'll be on the path of your own choosing.

When you're climbing a mountain and you reach a pass along the trail with a steep jump in elevation, with a lot of rocks and challenging steps in front of you, what do you look for? You look for the most level and secure surfaces to plant your feet or perhaps a nearby tree to hold on to for balance and stability. When you reach out for that tree, you may notice the bark isn't rough and scratchy because it has been smoothed by the many hands that have clung to it before.

Where have you encountered solid surfaces and handholds along the way? Who have been the grounded and inspirational members of your support network? When you answer these two questions, you're likely to identify critical points in the evolution of your career and your own personal development. Recognize the impact and influence that comes along with engaging environments filled with inspiring mentors and coaches.

Goal. Throughout this book you'll see a series of goal prompts. Are you in the habit of setting goals for yourself? Do you write them down? If you do, these exercises will work into existing goal-setting routines. If you have not developed a goal-setting routine, you'll be taking one of many actions that will help you live the life you want. Spend some time looking inward and reflecting on what fills up your cup. Identify the things that are essential and meaningful for you to have personal fulfillment. Set short- and long-term goals for your own personal frame of mind.

Now that we've gotten into a rockstar mindset, with personal commitment and conviction at its core, we're going to do some deep diving into tools, tactics, strategies, and processes that are essential for successful professional service marketing. While we do that, intention and mindset will remain at the center of everything we do.

2

Get Your Assets in Order

When it comes to brand, certain assets immediately come to mind, assets that most established businesses have in place: a logo, a website, a tagline, pictures, ads run over the years, and so on. No matter where you're starting from, whether you have fewer than a dozen files and a three-page website or hundreds of files and a massive website, your ability to keep marketing assets organized makes a tremendous difference in the quality and satisfaction of your work. As with most areas of business, assets and content accumulate over time, and marketing tends to be very file heavy.

We moved into our home three years ago, and for three years I haven't been able to find my kitchen mallet. It's big and clunky and doesn't fit in the cooking utensil drawer. When occasions popped up when I wanted to use it, I never took the time to do the deep search and locate it. Would it have made my life easier as I prepped our food? Of course. Would the dish have come out better had I used my mallet? Almost certainly. For three years certain dishes were just a little worse off because of my lack of organization. But as one would hope, things once misplaced do eventually turn up. Last week, while head first in a deep corner cupboard, my husband shouted out, "Hey, I found your mallet!"

We all have "mallets" at work. Hopefully, thoughtful file names enable our searches to lead us to our destination and physical assets are well organized too. Unfortunately, that is not always the case.

Digital Asset Management

So where to begin? Let's start with digital assets, as they tend to accumulate en masse within the marketing arena. Below is a list of folders and subfolders that set a solid foundation for long-term organization in your primary directory.

Advertising
    Digital Advertising
        Specific Media Partners (a subfolder for each one)
        Geofence Marketing
    Print Advertising
        Specific Media Partners (a subfolder for each one)
    Audio Advertising (including Radio)
    Video Advertising (including TV)
    Community Events
        Sponsorships
        Program Ads
        Specific Organizations (a subfolder for each one)
        Quotes – Contracts
Articles and Resources (training references)
Copywriting and PR
    Content Articles
    Press Releases
    Letters
    Media Directory – Contacts
Direct Mail and Printed Collateral
    Brochures
    Business Cards
    Product Sheets
Email Marketing
    Email Message Copy

Banner Ads

Email Lists

Events

Specific Events (a subfolder for each one)

Displays – Banners

Graphics (generally Adobe Creative Suite files)

Logo Files

Corporate Logos

Logos of Partner Organizations

Social Media Logos

Infographics

Style Guide

Web Graphics

Images (photographs)

Staff Headshots

Staff – Office Events

Stock Photos

Event Photos

Photo Shoots

Lists

Client Lists

Competition

Key Contacts

Industry Reports

Presentations

PowerPoint Templates

Business Units (a subfolder for each one)

Sales

Sales Sheets

Sales Training

Prospect Lists

Client Relationship Management Reports
Sales Metrics

Social Media
Social Media Editorial Calendar
Specific Platform (a subfolder for each one)
Analytics
Content
Advertising
Images (sized specifically for the platform)

Strategy and Planning
Strategic Planning
Budget – Financials
Vendor Contracts

Video
Staff Videos
Demos and How-To Videos
Event Videos
Promo Videos
Holiday Videos

Website
Analytics
Site Architecture
Page Content
Blog Content
Website Images

Search Engine Optimization

By no means is this outline fully comprehensive, but it provides a solid foundation and basis for organizing that has proven to be incredibly effective. Not only will this effort help you, but it will help others who need to step in and access files in the future.

Rookie Tip. If you are inheriting legacy files, whether 100 or 5,000, and there is little rhyme or reason as to how they are organized, don't get bogged down in trying to organize files you may never use. Your time is far better spent on other projects. Instead, pull out the most relevant files and add them to a new file directory. If file names are not helpful in identifying subjects, organize them into folders and rename the files. For example, if you have 25 image files from an event on December 1, 2018, the file names are likely 12012018_001.jpg, 12012018_002.jpg, and so on. Those file names will not help you stay organized, nor will they add any value when you upload the images to the Web. After you've identified a group of images that all belong to a specific event, highlight all of them, right click on one of them, and rename that file. Each file in that group will be assigned that name followed by a sequential number in parentheses. For example, if you rename a file to Marketing_For_Rookies_book_launch.jpg, you will end up with files named Marketing_For_Rookies_book_launch(1).jpg, Marketing_For_Rookies_book_launch.jpg(2), etc. Not only does this make your files searchable by the subject of their file name, it also creates keyword-specific file names that contribute to search engine optimization (SEO) when uploaded to the Internet.

One of the fantastic things about getting organized and building this practice into your routine workflow is that certain tasks, such as responding to a request for a logo from an advertiser, designer, or the organizer of an event, become quick and simple. The time saved in getting them what they need is time you can use to build the relationship with that person while in the midst of the exchange. Go that extra step when sending a file to someone by letting them know that if they need a different file type, have questions, or need anything adjusted, to please let you know. This way, you're not only serving as an additional resource, you're also setting the expectation that you want to be involved in how your brand assets are used.

Asset Development

In order to have asset files at your fingertips, they first need to be developed. How many times have you seen a logo on a brochure or web page and it looks all fuzzy, or the background is black or white when it should have been transparent? Understanding the nuances of which files to use and effectively engaging with your media partner to ensure a positive and on-point brand experience are skills that all marketers must develop. This is especially true for marketing generalists.

What if you don't have the file formats you need or the necessary software to create them? One thing that has remained consistent in all the years I've been in professional service marketing is that in-house marketing is often the responsibility of a generalist— a department of one. Whether you're taking on marketing responsibilities in additional to your primary role or you're just settling in as a new marketing professional, being a marketing generalist has a whole lot of upside, responsibility, and opportunity. You'll simply need to become fluent in the language of designers to the extent that you ensure proper file use. As you grow, you'll develop knowledge and strategic understanding in all areas of marketing. This is one of the most attractive and rewarding aspects of being a marketing generalist. You will rarely be bored, and there will always be new things to learn!

Working up a simple graphic file or overseeing image selection keeps the creative juices flowing. You'll also be able to quickly and easily resize any image or logo file and ensure your images for print are nice and crisp and your images for the Web are as crisp as they can be without slowing down your page load speed. The ability to manage this work in-house speeds up productivity exponentially. It also adds a valuable skill and source of inspiration to your quiver.

A consistent theme in this book is personal development and lifelong learning. When you want to acquire new skills, what do you do? You take a course, attend a webinar, or watch a how-to video and stock your workspace with the tools and software necessary to practice your trade. If you don't yet have the Adobe Creative Suite, make time in your schedule to watch some videos, review the features and pricing, and start thinking about all the ways you can use the applications. When requesting an investment in your workspace, offer examples of immediate uses and the return on investment for the software/equipment, time, and training. Doing so shows that you will put in the work necessary to gain mastery and increase efficiency. Plan on using (and saving for later reference) low-barrier resources such as the Adobe training tools and how-to videos on YouTube; both are full of easy-to-digest lessons that will get you going quickly. They are a smart time investment for an in-house marketing generalist and for the business.

Train your brain to think in terms of mastery. Will you develop advanced expertise in all things Adobe Creative Suite? Maybe, but not likely. But when you approach your work with the intent of mastery, no matter how broad the scope, you're starting with a success mindset. Whether learning how to properly size an image for use on the Web or pitching an upgrade to a fully loaded, graphics-capable PC for your workstation, approach your work with the conviction of a success mindset.

Let's go back to a specific point for just a moment. As a generalist you're developing a wide variety of skills and responsibilities. Own that. Embrace that. Marketing is incredibly strategic and analytical, but it is also very creative and fun. Many of us who gravitate toward this profession love this collision and consider it the best of both worlds. Whether you outsource the graphics work or you develop your skills over many years, find the balance that works well for you. But don't shy away from the creative side of the work altogether. If you do, it will be more difficult to develop and manage the personality of your brand. Remember, the creative elements of marketing are often rich sources of ingenuity and exploration.

I'll get more in depth about outsourcing and agency work later on, but whether resources are created in-house or outsourced, you're bound to generate a lot of drafts and versions of files. Keeping these organized will free up time and allow you to focus on more valuable work.

When it comes to technology, your workstation and other devices will very likely be quite different from other devices on the network. Perhaps the network is made up of thin clients all working off a shared server, and the majority of time is spent working on cloud-based software solutions. Most people are not accessing Facebook and YouTube at work, but those of us responsible for marketing may need to. Your work requires a computer with an enhanced graphics card, access to websites that may be blocked to other employees, two monitors for efficiency, audio and video features, and the hardware to run at top speed even with multiple installed applications and dozens of large files open. These sorts of details and assets may be new and unique for a business. After all, it is a wonderfully unique and exciting opportunity to be a marketing generalist within a professional service organization. In order to get the tools necessary to succeed, open a dialogue with your supervisor, a managing partner, or the business owner (whoever is champion of your advancement and success), and pull in your IT manager. If you outsource IT support, bring in someone from that company to discuss what sorts of technology assets are necessary for a workstation built specifically to support marketing and advertising activities. The technology needs of a marketing professional are very different from the technology needs and setup of others on an office network. Work with those who are in a position to help you put in place the tools you need to be successful.

Rookie Tip. Don't be afraid to ask for what you need, and don't ask for what you need without being prepared to explain why you need it. When an in-house marketing position is new or the predecessor had been managing marketing as a very low priority, you may be stepping into a setup that is less than ideal with regard to technology capabilities, organization, files on hand, and so on. Spend time out of the gate doing an audit of what you have available to you, and work with an IT colleague to identify what you need. Even if you phase in upgrades over time to get your workstation up to par, be a vocal advocate for investments in technology tools right of the gate. If you don't, all of your work going forward will be that much more difficult.

Goals. Implement a logical organizational structure to your marketing drive. Get your folders set up to house your files. Every time you finalize a file, give it a logical and accurate file name. Hold a meeting with your in-house IT expert, or request to hold a meeting with your outsourced IT support. Walk through an exercise of identifying what types of enhancements and investments should be made to your workstation to set you up for success. Be sure to cover hardware, software licenses, and access capabilities to Internet sites that may be blocked on the network. Make your IT expert a trusted advisor and resource. Once you have their recommendations, align the investments with the expected return and present your request to your supervisor or business owner. Remember, you've got this!

3

Marketing Budget

How many people balance their checkbook with a pen and calculator these days? The last time my husband and I did that was back in 2013. Of course, that doesn't mean we don't track money as it flows in and out of our accounts. We simply began using online banking, digital statements, and online bill pay. In many ways it's helpful to think of your marketing budget like you think of your personal banking. You keep track of bills being paid on time, ensure money is available when needed, reserve money for emergencies and planned purchases, and automate transactions, all the while closely monitoring activities.

We also do our own personal return on investment (ROI) analysis, sometimes without even realizing it. Every now and again we weight the value of adult-only time to go off and have a little adventure and romance. The return for all the planning and expense is worth every penny and ounce of effort. We spend money to enjoy a nice dinner, relax in a lovely hotel where we know a three-year-old won't be waking us up at 5:00 am, hit the trails for some adventuring on off-road Segways, and follow that up with a scenic chairlift ride and hike to the top of Sugarloaf Mountain. The return? Rejuvenation, connectedness, exercise, experience, fun, rest, and more.

The point is that when we choose to make investments, we do so with intention and commitment, knowing that we'll forever have the imprint of the experience in our memories.

How to Approach Budgeting

Branding campaigns, designed to build top-of-mind awareness, are sort of like paying your utility bills. It's something you need to do. Branding lets people know you're there. The marketing magic comes into play when branding campaigns are combined with strategic brand expcriences, like the weekend getaway with off-road Segways and scenic vistas. Strategically show your target market an advertisement, and they're going to know who you are. Move them to action through an emotion or an experience, and you're on your way to earning their trust and converting them into a client. Your role as the marketer is mapping out not only what these activities will look like but also when and where they occur and in what sequence. All of this takes planning and budgeting.

How many times have you filled out a registration form for a tradeshow, submitted an advertisement, ordered a couple thousand branded pens, sponsored an event, or boosted a Facebook post, only to wonder how that investment fits into the overall marketing budget? Asking those questions is a good thing; it shows that you are taking seriously the responsibility of stewarding resources. The quality of the questions you ask and the skills you develop will position you to do great things. Let me say that again: The quality of the questions you ask and the skills you develop will position you to do great things. Step into that curiosity and ownership of the responsibility. As you develop budgeting and financial management skills, pay close attention to what questions you ask. Listen and learn from those around you who are asking thoughtful, powerful questions. One of the first questions to ask is simply, "Is there a dedicated marketing budget?" Other questions that will help you build an understanding of the current financial process include, "How do we approach the annual budgeting process? May I participate? Will you please show me how this has been done in the past?"

Most businesses work through a budgeting process every year. There's little way around it. The owner and senior leadership may manage the process start to finish, department heads are sometimes responsible for managing their own budget, and staff may or may not be involved in the budgeting process. If you don't know how the process currently works, ask. Be committed to a mindset of mastery and conviction. When you're showing up as a thoughtful and responsible marketing professional, you elevate the importance of the work in your own sphere of influence, and you also ratchet up the commitment to marketing for the whole business. Both are very powerful and have great potential for long-term positive impact. Be comfortable in those shoes. Once you have them on, they can take you far.

Marketing, advertising, communications—these are all critical functions of every business. If the starting point is a couple of line items on the chart of accounts (COA), so be it. When you're solely or mostly responsible for activities that have expenses tied to them, it makes sense that you be part of the budgeting process.

The year-end planning and design of a budget that maps out activities for the following year is very important. So too is the ongoing month-to-month budgeting that helps tie activities and results to the approved budget. Throughout the course of the year you will track performance of specific activities and attribute outcomes to the cost of each investment. Without this crucial step, you're bound to repeat activities whether they have a neutral, negative, or positive result.

To understand how the business tracks expenses, you need to know the classifications for the COA. Every COA will have differences. Some are extremely detailed, while others include only the major categories of expense activities. Using the COA to open a dialogue with the business owner and/or finance manager will spark a great discussion about budgeting, expense allocation, and current processes. The environment may be very transparent, or not. You'll need to broach the subject to find out. Like most opportunities to step into more responsibility and leadership, the better prepared you are with information and thoughtful questions, the stronger your position will be to make an impact. Here are a few examples of expenses typically classified as marketing expenses in a COA:

Advertising
    Print, radio, TV, and digital advertisements
    Program ads (even those pitched as a sponsorship, if submitting an ad file)
    Google Ads (search/display)
Marketing
    Sponsorships and events (catering, event promotion, entertainment)
    Website development (design, SEO)
    Website domain and hosting fees
    Social media management
    Signage (community-based; a permanent sign at your location may be classified as a capital expense)
Consulting
    Concept/campaign/logo design
    Copywriting
    Agency and other support services
Referral and appreciation programs
Printing and reproduction
    Banners
    Business cards
    Flyers

Rack/postcards
Logo tablecloths
Giveaway items
Misc. (resides in other areas of the COA)
Training and seminars
Postage
Travel
Meals
Office supplies (including branded stationery)
Salary and benefits

You'll notice that I listed the salary and benefits expense separately. Depending on how detailed their budgeting process is, some companies allocate portions of salary and benefits to several departments, especially when someone has several primary responsibilities and is not fully focused on marketing. The other benefit of summing your total expense minus salary and benefits is so that you know how many resources are available for activities.

Tracking Expenses Over Time

Now that you have a list of what to include in your budget, two steps will help you get organized and also exhibit tremendous leadership. The first is using a dedicated tool to track your marketing expenses, and the second is your willingness and ability to work collaboratively with peers throughout the budgeting process.

The business owner, finance director, or chief financial officer (CFO)—that is, whoever manages the books for the company—has already established a COA to manage the finances.

A great question to ask is, "How much was spent last year for marketing?" Whether you manage the budget or you're moving in that direction, it is incredibly useful to look at a roadmap. Your prior-year expenses are your map.

That's not to say that you'll repeat everything you did last year, but there will always be some repeat expenses and activities that occur year after year. Maybe last year your office moved into a larger space, or you launched a new service. There are also many reasons for fluctuations from year to year. Knowing the annual allocation for marketing year to year is useful information for the person who manages marketing activities. If your business practices zero-sum accounting, each year the budget begins at zero and you build your plan and associated expenses with justifications for each activity. With this approach, it matters not what you spent last year, only what you intend to do this year. When having a discussion about budgeting and process, ask the finance manager questions about process and budget format. In many small businesses, department managers are granted the flexibility and encouragement to build their own spreadsheet to map out expenses, reporting the details to the senior leadership. It all goes back to asking good questions and taking the initiative.

So once you're on the path to developing a budget and roadmap of activities, the next question to answer is how to keep yourself and the marketing activities organized. You may have access to the books or an application to track a department budget. The complement to this, and the tool that will enable you to create your own working file and planning document, is an Excel spreadsheet. In larger organizations, department budgets are often built within a finance application. If this is the case, the Excel budget file is used as the planning and design tool in conjunction with the finance application, leaving you with access to details and an ability to shift activities as you track results and effectiveness. Formatting your budget with COA expenses in the first column and 12 months of expenses in the columns that follow allows for simple summing and tracking by rows and columns. I have developed and formatted tools, including a marketing budget template, that are available on my website (https://hillarydow.com/marketing-resources). Because isn't life just a whole lot easier when we ask for resources and a little help?

When you develop and refine these organizational tools with input from your finance manager, you'll create a win–win. They will see that you're taking the initiative to responsibly steward company resources, with the added bonus that you're doing so in alignment with current financial processes and COA classifications. You're also setting yourself up for better strategic planning. As you develop strategies to meet marketing goals, you will use your budgeting tool throughout the year.

As the months pass, I typically toggle between two tabs in my budgeting tool: the primary budget that maps out planned and available resources month to month and an ROI tool where I tie expenses invested in specific activities to value and cost per acquisition. Although my preference is to keep multiple tracking tools in one file or marketing dashboard, you'll determine what works best for you as you spend more time developing and using these sorts of tools. There are thousands of "martech" (marketing technology) tools on the market today. As you research these tools, you may see the term "martech stack." Think of the stack as the network architecture of all the technology used within your marketing department. Even the most modest marketing departments manage martech, so if the COA includes an information technology (IT) line, your department will allocate martech expenses to the IT account. This still resides in the marketing budget.

Most companies have strategic objectives that evolve annually, tying into long-term goals. Marketing strategies and campaigns are designed to support those goals. When you have an overall allocation of how much money is available in the marketing budget, why not embrace the responsibility of leveraging those dollars? Research, plan, and propose new and intentional activities, with the end in mind. How often do you propose new investments or new marketing activity?

What is it they say? Oh yes—if you continue doing what you've always done, expect to get the same result. Because simply maintaining the status quo is a dangerous way to run a business. Unless you're OK with losing market share, you've got to evolve by trying new things.

If you already have authority to manage the marketing budget and make buying decisions, that's fantastic. Not many start in that place though, unless you're also the owner and entrepreneur. If you do not yet have authority to make buying decisions, the path to that responsibility is through the thoughtful stewarding of current resources, communication and collaboration with the business owner or your supervisor, and tracking your results. When you tie your efforts back to results, you're making another notch in your marketing belt.

4

Breaking Old Habits

"**B**ut we've always done it that way." We've all heard this phrase. If not, you're likely in a business that looks forward more than it looks back and that is an absolutely awesome, super-amazing thing. History is important—without it we wouldn't learn lessons or be where we are today. But, let's be honest: The future is where it's at, and what we do today will define that future. Change is inevitable. Change is necessary to stay relevant. These statements are true of business and industry, and they are true of people. Here is a quote that is much more motivating:

"Be the change you wish to see in the world." —Mahatma Gandhi

Change starts with an idea. Ideas lead to action. Action leads to productivity. Productivity generates results. Results are analyzed. Analysis sparks refinement. Refinement enables improvement. Improvement generates success. Success spurs more ideas. Do you prefer these statements, or "We've always done it that way"? Unequivocally, without a doubt, be a champion of change!

Become a Champion of Change

Certain forces and circumstances are well beyond your control, but within your own spheres of influence you often have the ability to make an impact in deeply meaningful ways. When you focus and center your efforts on the essential projects, processes, and people, you can initiate and help make profound change.

27

The key to successful change is rooted in relationships and communication. As you are building your technical skills and industry knowledge, there must be as much emphasis (sometimes more) on building relationships. One way to consistently develop trust with the internal and external networks around you is through the exchange of information and ideas. Working together, having open dialogue, providing feedback, and detailing and explaining data and processes—these are ways that people learn and build relationships. When these things are happening, change is all but inevitable.

Humans are biologically designed to avoid danger via fight or flight. We often perceive change to be dangerous; therefore, it is human nature to resist change. So imagine how important it is to trust those leading change and how precious the relationships are for all parties involved. Leading others through change or participating in a change process, perhaps as the champion of communication or the go-to expert on creating messages and choosing communication channels, is a great responsibility with a tremendous amount of work. There is also a great deal of reward.

Sometimes the change is a shift in resources. For example, suppose a business has always advertised in the region's four telephone books but has not yet ventured into utilizing Google Ads. Bingo! Herein lies a tremendous opportunity for you to gather data that support the shift in looking at things differently. Just as important as a willingness to look at things differently, change happens with a willingness to allocate resources differently. A business owner will want to know why a change is recommended. Your ability to communicate why you are recommending a new or different marketing initiative, a new way of reaching your target market or crafting new messaging, will have a lot to do with your success in initiating change.

the In the phone book and Google Ads example, let's identify specific steps in that change process:

1. Discuss the historical process and "why" behind allocating resources to enhanced print advertising in four separate books.

2. Explain why you would like to explore and fully understand the relationship with the phone book vendor, so you can do a complete cost–benefit analysis.

3. Identify (make photocopies of) existing print advertisements.

4. Identify the current budget allocation for all four books.

5. Acquire the contact information for your advertising representative.

6. Identify which book (or books) in which you would automatically have a white- and yellow-page listing (i.e., those books covering areas in which you have a physical location).

7. Contact your advertising representative and identify the annual contract renewal date. Ask for pricing of various options in each of the books. Different markets produce different-sized books based on population, and size drives the prices. Also ask about digital online directory services, including their own online directory, as well as managing the accuracy of your listing across the landscape of online directories. This service is at the core of how phonebooks have evolved with technology.

8. Phone books now offer an opt-out option, so when you ask for the total circulation of each book, ask them if they will also provide the impact opt-outs have had on circulation.

It does not escape me that some of my readers will ask, "What is a phone book?" Back in the day, before cell phones and the Internet, when everyone had a landline telephone connected to a phone jack in the wall, you would thumb through a big old book containing an alphabetical listing of people and businesses and their phone numbers in the white pages and a category-based list of businesses in the yellow pages. The yellow pages include text directories as well as display advertising. An enhanced listing in the yellow pages may include extra bold or color in the text column or a display ad elsewhere on the page. The phonebook is still automatically delivered to your door, and, as you can imagine, the size of the book has consistently shrunk over the past two decades.

If your business was established many years ago, the likelihood that you placed advertising in the yellow pages at some point is very high. In years past, it was the go-to resource when you wanted to call someone or contact a business. Now, people use the Internet, and most consider their smart devices an extension of themselves.

But enough about history. Let's get back to how you position data, trends, and projections to drive change. Because, yes, some businesses still place display advertising in printed telephone books. Some businesses leverage digital tools offered by the yellow pages and in doing so will have a print ad thrown into their annual contract at no additional expense. These are the types of negotiations with an advertising vendor that add value and reach to your marketing activities.

If you use a dedicated tracking number in a listing or advertisement, whether in print or online, you can easily tie the volume of phone calls back to that specific phone number. Most small businesses do not get into this level of sophistication or added expense. Working with your online directory vendor will gain you access to call volume reports and other analytics. As with all vendors, or media partners as I like to call them, it is wise to maintain a good relationship and keep lines of communication open. Even better, hold them accountable for providing analytics and performance reports.

All small businesses may claim their business listing through Google My Business. There you are able to view insights that track how many people clicked to call your phone number, viewed the map to your location, and more. Keeping a strong relationship with your yellow pages account manager will enable you access call volume reports from their online directories. As you track various channels, the more informed you'll be on which activities are performing well. The more you learn about channels (the various formats and delivery methods for your messages), the stronger your position will become to move the needle on change.

I began this chapter with the statement, "We've all been there." And I have been there, many times. The more you grow and volley in your career, the more change you're bound to encounter. Nowhere was this more true than during my time in healthcare marketing, in a climate of tremendous, sweeping change.

Leaders set the tone as positive change agents. Some people have the enviable fortune of working alongside truly exceptional leaders during their career. I placed myself in this group while working in healthcare, and I am a stronger and wiser professional because of it.

With an outward emphasis on promoting service lines and generating business for the health system, there was a tenable and immediate need to maintain a watchful and very engaged eye inward, with focus on internal stakeholders. When in the middle of rapid and significant change, staffing and retention become priorities in all industries, especially in a highly skilled service environment during a time of historically low unemployment.

By focusing on immediate and simple changes such as reformatting the employee e-newsletter to increase communication and engagement, supporting the human resource department with communications for service excellence initiatives, collaborating with senior leadership to launch an internal podcast filled with inspiration and information, and stepping up staff and community engagement with social media as a tremendous resource and two-way communication tool, my marketing team made significant impacts.

Were there channel limitations and bumps along the way as we tried new things? Of course. But by remaining focused on why we were trying so many new things—that is, supporting the people in our organization—the inevitable trial and error was worth it every single time. We even used a caricature of our CEO within our service excellence communications to help cut through the clutter, connect with staff, and humanize efforts in a way that added a bit of fun to often weighty, difficult subjects.

At the core of professional service businesses are the people that give their talents, time, personality, and emotions. The people are the business. When it comes to change, is it easier to change a lightbulb or change the minds and behaviors of a human being? If you haven't yet worked through the challenges and thrills of this question, welcome to professional services marketing and communications. You're in for all sorts of opportunities to grow and flex those development muscles.

Habits are entrenched in people as much as they are in cultures. Don't be afraid to be a lone wolf if you believe there is potential to make a positive impact. Here are a few pointers to remember when initiating and helping guide others through change:

1. Speak up and make a reasoned case for why the change is worth making, accepting input and ideas from many as you map out steps and tactics in your strategy.
2. Be kind, open, and honest with people. Never underestimate how important and powerful these qualities are in business and in life.

3. Remain diligent with analysis and follow-up and always stay adaptable yourself as the change rolls out. Be a change leader.

Another force for change in the marketing world ties in with strategy and execution. Areas that often become entrenched in habit include media buys, stale creative materials for advertising, sponsorships without strategy, events without follow-up, phone book advertising without social media, and so on. My guess is that you see at least one thing here that you would put on your "we've always done it that way" list. But do you know what I love about lists? You can scrap them in an instant and make yourself a new list. Of course, change is never that simplified. But you can identify items to tackle first, then make calculated changes, and, when you begin to see results, have something to point to as proof of the value in evolving how you approach marketing.

How you slice and dice the design of omnichannel campaigns (campaigns that run across multiple channels) becomes the special sauce in your strategies. No chef would ever spread the same sauce over every dish on the menu. Who wants balsamic reduction on their chicken piccata?

When you identify the goal—perhaps to increase new clients brought through the door, build brand recognition in new markets, or enhance the services provided to existing clients—you need to approach it with fresh eyes and the willingness to apply new and different tactics to achieve the specific goals. When you don't, when you entrench and do things as you've always done them, you had better be prepared for an erosion of the status quo and increasing irrelevancy. Eventually, status quo slides into decline in a variety of ways.

Tap Into the Stream of Information

So many thought leaders in marketing and business are rockstars when it comes to sharing new trends to watch, how-tos, case studies, podcast interviews with pioneers across industries, and more. So much is changing all the time, with so many things to learn. The great thing is that information is right at your fingertips. One of the best decisions you can make for your career and your own development is to commit to consuming new and well-developed content. Otherwise, how will you be able to keep up with change?

What do you read on a daily basis? Whose headlines do you follow? What podcasts do you listen to? Do you observe how your competitors are advertising across multiple channels? Where is your target market going to consume content? Do you click on sponsored ads to research new tools, access studies and guides, and learn new trends in your market? If you're struggling to answer these questions, then you're going to love this identified goal.

> **Goal.** Over the next six months, research and explore a variety of content providers and identify a few favorites. Build time into every day to read something, attend a webinar, or plan a call with a vendor to learn about how they solve problems. Make consumption of information part of your daily routine.

Once you've joined an email list, read the emails regularly. When they offer a free article, click on it, download a copy to your articles folder, or bookmark the URL in an articles folder to build a go-to library of content that will be at your fingertips when you have a window of time for focused reading. In addition to increasing your knowledge, you'll also begin to identify niche leaders you may want to work with to support your own marketing strategy.

Here are a few of my favorite resources, thought leaders, media outlets, trade associations, and other content providers that I learn from often:

- Social Media Examiner
- American Marketing Association
- Digital Today
- Search Engine Land
- HubSpot
- Inc.
- Forbes
- LinkedIn

Even with what often feels like an overload of priorities, commitment to learning and changing with the evolution of marketing and industry is an absolute must.

A colleague once gave me an old-school tin button that had "we've always done it that way" inside a red circle with a giant slash across it. He gave it to me soon after I joined the team, and though I didn't wear it on my lapel every day, I did pin it to my bulletin board within direct eyesight of my monitors. Visual reminders, sharing quotes at the beginning of meetings or team huddles, following inspirational bloggers, reading and learning about new things, trying, doing, experimenting—however you do it, venture into the new. Don't be afraid to pitch an idea, spice up some content, jazz up a staff event, or change ad copy. Don't let fear or hesitancy about change hold you back. The more you explore, learn, and thoughtfully execute, the more progress you will make.

5

Clients . . . Where are you?

This question comes up a lot. Where do I find new clients, and how do I engage with them? One truth we all face is that the evolution of technology has changed consumer behavior. People are connected to their devices, and as a marketer you need to understand how this impacts consumer behavior. The days of a linear sales funnel are rapidly disappearing, and the dawn of personalized consumer journeys has arrived. People increasingly expect you to understand who they are and what they want, and when they are looking for your service or product, they want to find it fast. People want value and information, they want time savers and expertise, and these things lay the foundation for building awareness and trust. Let's cover the basic steps:

1. Define your client persona—in great detail.
2. Create brand awareness by mapping and understanding the buying journey.
3. Build authority as someone they know, like, and trust.
4. Closely align marketing, advertising, and sales.
5. In professional services, leverage referrals and personal introductions.

Client Persona

Everywhere you look, you may be seeing prospects and future clients around every corner. How do you get in front of them? How do you land a meeting with a decision maker? Would they be a good fit for your services?

The first challenge is to focus on a specific target market, one that you have a track record of success with, one that you've been proven to be a great match for time and time again. So let's dig in.

When you look through your client list, begin by answering the following questions. Think about the business as a whole, and if the question applies to the makeup of your business, also think in terms of clients managed by individuals within your business.

- What are the industries and demographics that you see high volumes of?
- Are you serving a lot of clients in the retail sector, farming and agriculture, hospitality, or healthcare?
- Do you have a defined niche? Multiple niches?
- Do you have a strong presence in specific towns?
- Have you saturated your local market?
- Is there more opportunity in the surrounding regions?
- Are your clients typically younger or older?

As you work through answering these questions, guess what? You're digging into market analysis! Looking inward has the potential to yield a treasure trove of information and is critically important. What are you exceptionally good at? Whom do you and the staff easily and meaningfully connect with? Many times our niches develop out of organic and unintentional growth. Before you know it, you've developed little pockets of industry expertise. The more specific you are in defining who makes up your current client base, or audience, the more effective your efforts will be in growing that specific niche.

Really think about who you're targeting. It is very common in professional services to fall into the trap of throwing a very broad and generic net, trying to reel in any and all businesses or customers within your geographic footprint. Resist this temptation. When you direct your marketing at everyone, you run the risk of connecting with very few. When your creative materials are designed to appeal to a very specific group, you set targeting parameters, and your ad placement goes directly to members of your identified audiences, you will see results.

Here is a list of questions that will help you narrow in on a very specific client persona. Start with identifying only a couple of target personas. Beginning with a very narrow and specific target audience will keep you focused.

1. Are they male or female?
2. How old are they?
3. What is their typical job title?
4. Do they stay at home or work in a business?
5. Are they married? Do they have children?
6. Do they have a college education?
7. Do they play a sport? What sport? Did they play a sport in high school?
8. Do their children play sports?
9. Do they frequent local entertainment venues (stadiums, ballfields, golf courses)?
10. Do they frequent the local arts scene (galleries, museums, theaters, concert halls)?
11. Do they like to socialize, or do they prefer staying in?
12. Do they like to go shopping or do they prefer buying items online?
13. Do they like to travel?
14. Do they use public transportation, or do they always drive themselves?
15. Do they own their own home?
16. Do they save for retirement?

These questions may seem pretty specific, but this level of detail will help you find and connect with people you've identified as the ideal target audience for your business. If you serve both business-to-business (B2B) and business-to-consumer (B2C) clients, identify a persona for each target. A law practice, for example, may have some lawyers specializing in family law and other lawyers specializing in corporate litigation. The target audiences are entirely different, resulting in very different client personas. To clearly understand how to build awareness, authority, and trust with a specific audience, we need to understand who they are in great detail.

Let's illustrate this with a very specific example. Meet the Clark family. Charlotte is an entrepreneur and employer, wife and mother of two. Charlotte is married to Allen, the CFO of the region's largest microbrewery. Charlotte is a parent, and she spends her days running her own local business, a successful café and bakery that is loved by the community. Allen, a lifelong lover of microbrews, landed his dream job as the CFO of a growing brewery that stands shoulder to shoulder with leaders and pioneers in the booming craft brew industry. With a master's degree in finance and a Certified Management Accountant certification, Allen loves learning and finance as much as he loves the craft of a good brew. Prior to joining the brewery, Allen was the controller of a national food manufacturer, headquartered in their hometown. Although Allen still travels occasionally for work, he was previously out of town on business travel up to 50% of the time throughout the year. The Clark family are all thrilled to have Dad home much more often.

Charlotte and Allen's children are both teenage athletes: Tommy plays football and Zoe is on the swim team. As working parents, both Charlotte and Allen cherish the time they have in the stands and at the pool watching their kids' sporting events. When attending a game or a swim meet, they do their best to be fully present. Cell phones are put away, and the pressures and deadlines of work are pushed aside until the next day. Their attention is on their child on the field or in the pool and the one sitting next to them in the stands. While at the Friday night football game, they pore through the program to see Tommy's picture, bio, and stats, review the upcoming schedule, and browse the local businesses who advertise and offer words of encouragement. As they watch Tommy throw a perfect spiral in a fifty-yard Hail Mary to win the game, Zoe captures the video on her cell phone while Charlotte and Allen are jumping and hollering beside her. In that moment, life is perfect.

Everything that contributed to Tommy getting to that point in time, that accomplishment, is part of a journey that proves the age-old adage that it takes a village to raise a child—or, in this case, a talented football player. Charlotte and Allen both appreciate and recognize the time and money contributed by coaches, boosters, local business sponsors, the school, and the community of cheerleaders who have all aided in providing Tommy the opportunity to soar.

> **Rookie Tip.** If you want to reach a dedicated parent of a student-athlete—if you want to be in front of Charlotte and Allen and connect with them on a personal level—find out the sponsorship, signage, and program advertising opportunities to support the local football team. Discounting or ignoring this often low-cost, high-emotion opportunity to connect with your target market is frequently overlooked by local businesses.

When Charlotte is not focused on her family, she is running a successful café and bakery that is a favorite of locals and students from the area colleges. The hot spot offers counter food service, fabulous coffees and teas, locally sourced produce and groceries, and also exceptional baked goods. Charlotte launched her business three years ago, and it has steadily grown year over year, now employing 12 people full-time.

Both Allen and Charlotte represent B2B as well as B2C client personas for a variety of professional services.

Brand Awareness

Given your services, are you targeting your immediate city, state, or region or are you seeking national clients, maybe even global? Many small businesses focus on local and statewide geographic targets.

Time and time again, a thoughtful mix of new and traditional media will lay a solid foundation for building brand awareness and generating leads. Here are key components in building brand awareness, moving a prospect to a lead, and converting them to a client:

- Ensure your market knows that you exist.
- Clearly identify what services you offer.
- Explain the problems and pain points you help clients overcome.
- Provide proof of your work and outcomes.
- Make it easy for someone to contact you.

As you design strategy around building awareness of your brand (that is, your business), always keep your audience in mind. Branding messages, creative concepts, and placement will stand a chance of being effective only if they reach and resonate with your target audience.

You pour your heart and soul into your business and into your career. But there are only so many hours in a day. The more strategic you are with your time and resources, the more return you'll have on that investment. When you think outside the box and connect in a meaningful way that offers value, you're bound to be noticed and make connections.

Digital marketing provides numerous ways to reach members of highly specified target markets. One popular method is geofence marketing. Think of geofencing as a location-specific digital targeting tactic, providing advertising impressions to members of your target audience based on their physical location. A digital fence is placed around a location, and mobile devices within the defined location are targeted. The device must have the location GPS tracker enabled. This is a high-level explanation, but it gives you the general idea.

Let's say I sell life insurance and I want to get my brand in front of the Clark family after they had their children. I know that certain occasions or periods in life (such as parenthood) heighten people's openness to brand resonance. I know that their buying journey for acquiring and adjusting life insurance likely shifted with the addition of children, and I also might surmise or even know that Charlotte and Allen take the kids into a professional photographer's studio for portraits and holiday pictures. (More and more photographers have a very mobile and location-agnostic approach these days, but those infant sessions still occur in a studio environment.) If Charlotte begins seeing advertising for life insurance appear on her photo-sharing app immediately following their infant's adorable portrait session, and the ad creative draws a strategic connection between growing families and the importance of life insurance, that ad is being delivered to the right person, at the right time, in a powerful way.

To strengthen the impact of the digital advertising, it is helpful when ad recipients have a personal connection with you or your agency. In this example, I would ask myself, "Have we connected over coffee and eggs at a Chamber of Commerce breakfast? Do my fellow employees and I patronize Charlotte's coffee shop? Does my agency sponsor Tommy's football team? Did I attend the grand opening of Allen's brew pub? Did I send a note of congratulations when the brew pub opened?" Herein lies the collision of traditional and new marketing.

Another example from my own past work includes geofence marketing for an orthopedic practice by placing a digital fence around golf courses and gyms. With a significant volume of patients who suffer from repetitive motion injuries, such as golfers and weight lifters, targeting visitors to those two types of business locations provided delivery of our advertising directly to the core of our target audience. Did it work? We exceeded annual growth and revenue goals and consistently increased new patient appointments month over month. Strategic marketing works. When you combine a targeting tactic such as geofencing with multiple layers of marketing and promotion, you too will develop your own expertise and see real results!

But I didn't just hit a magic button and start a geofencing campaign. I spent time learning about how it works and how it might fit into the other marketing activities in the overall strategy. I leveraged the relationship with one of our many media partners to layer geofencing into a broader digital advertising campaign. By specifically targeting a portion of the display network advertising, we placed our ad impressions in front of thoughtfully identified client personas. Yes, this work takes time, planning, and understanding, but you can do it too! Just keep adding skills and understanding to your quiver and lean on the expertise and resources of your media partners, and over time you too will be shooting arrows that are on message and on point.

Event marketing, a more traditional marketing approach, is a tried-and-true way to gain valuable face-to-face time with business owners, industry leaders, and prospects. Some events are geared toward learning and making peer connections, which are incredibly valuable, and other events are designed to serve as lead-generation opportunities. There is often crossover between the two, and both tap into your ability to be social and to build and to strengthen relationships.

After representing one of my employers at a traditional B2B trade show, I looked through the business cards that were collected at our booth. I then reviewed the cards and marketing collateral I'd collected while walking around the exhibit hall and talking with nearly all the other exhibitors. Both stacks of business cards were valuable, but in slightly different ways. With a colleague stationed at the booth, answering questions, handing out branded giveaways, and collecting lead contact information, I was maximizing time and opportunity by walking around to all the other booths. Everyone at a tradeshow wants to make connections—that's why you invest time and financial resources in the event. So do just that. Put your comfortable walking shoes on and really work the room. Zipping up and down the aisles and dropping cards in the fishbowls doesn't gain much more than a few chances at some door prizes. But slowly walking through and really engaging in conversation with the other exhibitors is where the gold is. Make memorable, meaningful connections. Always remember, someone may not need your services today (or they might), but you absolutely want them to think of you when the time comes that they do need your services.

But are events valuable only if they are face-to-face? Absolutely not! Does the event have a digital presence? Is there a digital pass? Is a hashtag being used at the event? If so, check out who is posting about the event. Like, comment on, and engage with their social media posts and make new connections through the digital experience tied to the event. You can even do this if you're not physically attending an event. For example, if Allen and his industry peers attend a microbrewers' symposium that draws in 200 of your state's serious microbreweries for networking and education, and you want to connect with that audience, engage with the event attendees in creative ways. Did you know that you can place a geofence around an event? You can. The fence is placed around the event venue, and when the mobile devices of the attendees are targeted, you're able to deliver ads to the app network of that device for 30 days. Think about that for a moment. Once the event is over, continue to cultivate contacts and prospects online. Send customized connection requests on LinkedIn asking to connect. Search Twitter for new contacts and follow their feed.

Think about how you get your brand in front of your target audience. There are very robust and strategic ways to do this. I challenge you to not let the fear of the unknown get in your way. Try new things, add new layers to your mix, and you will see results!

Keep going back to building and strengthening your skillset and understanding. Although it is impossible to do everything yourself, as you gain knowledge you will also gain confidence. This combination will lead you through strategic conversations with your media partners, internal stakeholders, prospects, and more. Focus on your own development while at the same time surrounding yourself with trusted, skilled, and supportive people. This sort of commitment and professionalism will serve you as well as the brand does. Through measured and thoughtful acts of professionalism, you yourself are a walking, talking, and shining representative of the brand.

Build Authority

When you want someone to purchase your expertise, knowledge, and services, most people with buying authority for a business or a home are going to have standards when choosing vendors and service providers. It is also often true that people want to do business with those they know personally, people they like and trust, or someone they are referred to by someone they know and trust.

Authority and experience take time to acquire, but actions can be taken to enrich the process as time goes by:

- Join a board or committee of a strategic organization.
- Volunteer for and organize speaking engagements.
- Write articles and blog posts.
- Join your professional organization.
- Embrace personal development; earn an advanced degree or certification.
- Always be ethical and uphold commitments.

Whether you are just starting out or have years of experience under your belt, nonprofit organizations are always seeking volunteers to join committees and the board of directors. Boards who approach volunteer recruitment strategically identify needed skills and experience that board members would bring to the organization, and they fill positions based on skill, character, expertise, and commitment to the organization's mission.

Volunteerism is a win-win-win proposition. The organization gains, you gain personally, and the business gains through your service as an ambassador serving on behalf of the business. Once an opportunity is identified that you are interested in, do research on the makeup of the organization and current board members. If you know any board members, ask them about their experience. The executive leadership and board president also serve as great resources when you are inquiring about joining a board or committee.

I myself have served on multiple boards and committees, even rising to the responsibility of board president and committee chair. Some of my strongest professional relationships and dearest friendships were born out of volunteerism. Give to others selflessly, and the return and reward will come back to you in the most profound ways. Having a quid pro quo approach is not the way to leverage volunteerism. That is also not a wise way to build authority.

I dare say you will hurt your reputation and decrease authority when you operate that way. Helping others and giving of your time and talents is where professional integrity aligns with gaining valuable experience, with the byproduct of building authority and expertise.

Two key differentiators of ongoing volunteer commitments rest in the organizational structure. Does the organization have a full-time staff executing the objectives and mission of the organization on a day-to-day basis? Or is the organization run entirely (or nearly entirely) by volunteers? This distinction is critically important when evaluating the true level of time commitment. When advising and offering a supportive role based on your expertise, you are providing time that is multiplied by work being done by internal staff. When you are helping to set strategy and also grinding out the functional operation tasks to keep an organization running, you will often be faced with a much higher level of time commitment. Both scenarios offer their own value; you just need to have an understanding of what you are committing to.

Let's take a closer look at that word, *commitment*. One of the *Oxford Dictionary*'s definitions is "an engagement or obligation that restricts freedom of action." Think about that for a moment. Now ask yourself why you are thinking about joining a board in the first place. Is it to give back to a cause you believe in? Do you want to gain experience while also giving back? Are you trying to make business connections? Whatever the reasons, and there are often many, it is important that you also view these sorts of commitments as just that—commitments. The ways in which you live up to these commitments inform others of how you manage your time and how you approach obligation. When circumstances change and a commitment is more than you bargained for, or you find that you simply do not have the capacity to uphold a commitment as originally intended, there is nothing wrong with that. It happens all the time.

The key is how you handle what you do next. In some cases it may just mean that you communicate with the leadership team and determine a new level of commitment if you wish to stay involved with the organization. Other times, you may need to step down with a graceful resignation. When you evaluate the reasons underlying volunteer commitments, they should align with the goals you've set for best managing your time and achieving your greatest possible contribution. What was once a meaningful and well-timed opportunity that struck a balance between professional experience and personal fulfillment may evolve into a mismatch with your goals. Or something as straightforward as a promotion at work and a dramatic increase in travel may make local commitments difficult to uphold. Whatever the case, when circumstances change, remember that how you handle the exit from a commitment is as important as how you contribute while volunteering.

Sometimes you are the volunteer and you are making these considerations and determinations for yourself. Other times you are serving as an advisor and coach to colleagues within your organization. Don't be afraid to advise. Ask yourself (or your advisees) thoughtful questions:

- How is your appointment to the board going?
- Have you made some meaningful connections?
- What has been the most rewarding part of your time this far?
- What has been the biggest challenge?
- Have you been attending each of the board meetings? If not, why?
- Have you joined a committee? Is there opportunity to head up a committee?
- When there is a major event, do you commit it to your schedule and attend?

The answers to these questions help identify when you're taking ownership of the commitment and making the most of volunteer opportunities. Remember, by investing time, energy, and expertise, you are doing a great service to an organization of your choosing as well as gaining an opportunity to build valuable experience.

Volunteerism is something to be proud of. It helps align you with others who share a passion for similar causes or a shared appreciation for giving back. You'll notice that professional bios often include volunteer activities and professional memberships. Be sure that both are included in the bios for you and your team.

LinkedIn Tip. There is a section on LinkedIn profiles called "volunteer experience." There you can list volunteer activities, and by selecting the appropriate business page, you can link your experience directly to the business page of the organization. As with the work experience and education sections, when you begin typing the name of the business, school, or organization, LinkedIn will start populating a dropdown list of pages with the same name. By selecting the correct one, you will create a link between your page and theirs. With this link, LinkedIn will identify people with whom you have common work experience, members of your alma mater, and so on. This is a great way to document and promote your experience and accomplishments.

Another great way to build authority is to offer resources through blog posts and articles to clients and prospects while exhibiting your knowledge and expertise and adding mad SEO power to your website. When you consistently post new articles to a blog, you are essentially sending up a flare to Google and other search engines that you are there and providing useful information. We'll get into SEO a bit in the next chapter, but don't worry, this won't turn into a tech manual.

Clients. . . Where are you?

Like most marketers in professional services you're probably saying to yourself, "But I am not a CPA (or a lawyer, dentist, chiropractor, you fill in the blank). How could I possibly write articles about topics I am not the expert in?" Don't worry, you can always hire services and agencies that specialize in content creation. It comes at a price, but the prices are reasonable and when you use the content wisely, you earn a return on the investment. This is an item to advocate for in your marketing budget.

When you build a library of useful articles, you can use them to pitch a column to your local newspaper, use as tools at lead-generation groups, add value to existing clients, and execute on your SEO strategy.

Here is a roadmap of how articles can be leveraged multiple ways:

1. Focus on sourcing articles of relevant topics, ones you know your target audience will find interesting and useful. To cut through the clutter, it's got to be relevant and well presented.

2. When acquiring content from a second party, make a few refinements so the article becomes your own. Add a bit of detail that is location specific (this is great for SEO). Work with one of your experts to add a real-life example to the article. Add hyperlinks to resources that will help readers find additional relevant information. These can and should also include internal links—that is, links to other pages within your own website.

3. When adding an article to your website, be sure to optimize the content for search engines using SEO. Use proper heading tags and include internal links to service pages of your website. Properly describe the article in the page title, creating a URL with strategic keywords. Use the targeted keywords in the page description. Include a strong and eye-

catching featured image, one that is relevant to the topic of the article. When you share the article on social media, this is the image that will appear. Remember, creative elements matter. All of these steps take time, but they add up to incredibly strong and valuable SEO. Spend the time working through these steps!

4. Once your article is properly formatted on your blog, include a teaser block in your email marketing and drive those users from their email inbox back to your blog.

5. With consistent posts to your blog, it becomes exponentially easier to make consistent article posts to your social media profiles. Choose a day of the week as your article day on social media.

6. Once your top-performing articles are identified, print out a few color copies on high-quality paper and use them to provide additional value (sometimes referred to as "value adds") when at lead-generation/referral groups and target-rich events. Think about your audience with this one. Some people love to consume content on paper. Just make sure your high-value content is printed on high-quality paper.

7. There may be an opportunity to submit your best performers to your local newspaper. If you pitch a recurring column of topics you've identified as homeruns with your audience, they'll consider it. If you are also an advertiser with the paper, even better!

As you can see, there is a lot of work to be done but also a lot of ways that you can leverage expert articles. Sometimes you have an expert on your team who loves to write. This is fantastic and a great opportunity for both of you to shine. Help them identify and focus on topics that people are interested in reading. What articles tend to have the highest open rates (that is, which articles are most opened and read)? What are the most frequently visited pages and blog posts of your website? When you search for terms in your industry in a keyword planning tool (such as Google's Keyword Planner), what are the most relevant keywords? These are all ways to identify hot topics for blog posts. When you've settled on a topic, help your colleague write in a way that will be easy and quick to consume. They may have written scholarly articles back in college, but when it comes to marketing you can help them tailor their writing style to speak to their target market.

Rookie Tip #1: Don't frustrate in-house content experts. When you do have an in-house expert step up to write an article, be sure to have a good discussion about the topic and intended audience. Even go so far as to describe Charlotte and the upcoming swim meet for Zoe. Make sure they are writing to your intended audience right from the get-go. Also dig into topic brainstorming. They will have awesome insights on topics they see over and over with clients. Then you can research which of these topics include the most desirable keywords in search engines. Validate their topics by running them through the keyword planner. Gauging interest via existing search volume and comparing your topics to content shared by others in your industry are useful steps to stay on track with the relevancy of your content. Not only will doing so make their article more successful in the long run, it will also save a lot of frustration and time if they are not pouring hours into an article written for the entirely wrong audience.

Rookie Tip #2: Format your articles for search engines. When you are consistently adding content to your website, the search engines notice. They notice because you use the necessary code to ensure your content is yelling at them through a megaphone via the title, page description, headings, relevant links, and so on. If all you do is paste the article onto the page and click "post," you will lose a tremendous amount of return. Search engines use words, images, headings, links, reviews, and more to determine whether to recognize your site as the authority. When someone sees your site at the top of the search results page and they click on your site, you've just gained an organic visitor. I've consistently seen organic site traffic deliver high volumes of users and, most important, users who take a desired action once on the site. When a desired action is taken, you've achieved a conversion! Slow down and take the time to optimize your articles. It is worth the time.

Rookie Tip #3: Write your own blog, now. With more available time and a flood of new experiences early on in your marketing career, devote some of your energy to a blog of your own. It doesn't need to be fancy, but it is a great way to develop and document your own expertise and experience.

Boost Confidence: Your Own and Others'

When you are looking inward or supporting those around you, be a champion of recognitions, personal development, training, public speaking opportunities, employee wellness—things that boost self-confidence, knowledge, and authority. Understand who in your business is a member of professional organizations; know what degrees and licenses people have. Getting this information organized packs a pretty powerful punch. Let me tell you why.

When people are entrenched in the day-to-day work of running the business, tending to clients, and prepping for the next day and next big project, it is very easy to allow training, development, and peer interaction to fall to the wayside. Luckily, for those in certified professions, ongoing education requirements force the practice upon them. It is beneficial to have a governing element within a profession that ensures skills and knowledge remain fresh and current with shifts in industry and the economy, so hopefully people view mandatory education as a great opportunity rather than a burden.

The more you understand the requirements of training and development, the better positioned you'll be to help fill in the gaps and support fellow employees who embrace voluntary training because it is part of the culture around them.

Does this become self-serving? Well, you're a member of the team, aren't you? Pushing for training, development, and professional memberships for employees across the board will only strengthen an organization and everyone in it, you included. Ensuring everyone has the tools and skills to operate at their very highest potential is the responsibility of every individual and every employer. When working together, that's when the magic happens.

Rookie Tip. When you're buried in work, your inbox is always bursting at the seams, and you just can't get ahead of the workload, it is very easy to put off training, again and again. Don't fall into this trap. If no one is holding you accountable for training, hold yourself accountable. Place dedicated blocks of time in your schedule for training, and don't be afraid to ask for membership fees to a professional organization that will help you develop skills and expertise. Be of service to others and to yourself.

We've covered a lot of material that looks inward, in a chapter focused on finding and attracting new clients. The strength of your team has a direct and powerful impact on your ability to attract clients and your position in the market. You need to be visible, trustworthy, expert, and memorable. Achieving these goals requires much internal work as well as outbound marketing and lead-generation activities.

6

Digital Marketing

Having a solid Web presence and digital strategy is paramount. Digital channels add tremendous value to your marketing efforts. Don't get discouraged if you're really starting from scratch; many small businesses are. Or perhaps you've got a website that has been sitting out there for a while and looks like it was built a decade ago (maybe it was).

Your website and digital strategy are areas that you can dig into quickly and easily to find many ways to truly shine. The ability to quantify and track results makes the time and dollars invested easy to tie directly to return.

Digital marketing encompasses so many things that it can very easily become overwhelming. As you find your way along the path, remember three very important points:

1. Your commitment to continuous learning paired with daily action *will* garner results. Don't let overwhelm intimidate you. Keep moving forward.

2. Don't be afraid of mistakes. In digital marketing you have so much data at your fingertips that you can and will identify blunders and correct them. As long as you learn from your mistakes, you've gained from the experience.

3. People specialize in singular slices of the digital marketing pie. As your strategy develops, surround yourself with experts who bring invaluable experience and unique skills to the table.

Digital Strategy

Why you choose to do something will always frame how you ultimately move forward with action steps. When the goal is to land more consultations and ultimately bring on Charlotte × 30 as clients this year, there must be a strategy for how you'll get to that end goal. Digital is a part of that strategy, a constantly increasing part.

Let's use Zoe and Charlotte as two examples of very different personas, each setting the stage for uniquely different buying journeys and user experiences. Zoe's digital footprint is going to look very different from her mom's; her searches will be different, and the ways she enjoys consuming and using technology will be very different. Understanding that and learning insights into how your target personas experience digital content sits at the center of your digital strategy.

Let's stick with Charlotte as our prospect and walk through setting a digital strategy for a law practice. Our goal is to have Charlotte make an appointment for a will and testament to be drawn up for her family, with advance directives. Charlotte and her husband have two children, they own their own home but carry a mortgage, both are college educated with remaining school loan debt, both contribute to their retirement accounts, both have college savings plans for the kids, and both have well-paying professional jobs. This all sounds very tidy and put together, right? They are responsible with their money and know they need to have wills in place, but they simply haven't made the time to take care of this task. This scenario is true for many families, presenting a great opportunity for law practices to build foundational relationships with families like Charlotte's.

Even at this level of detail, priorities and goals must always remain at the center of your thinking, planning, and executing. The creative elements carefully selected for promotions must also take all of these persona details into consideration. Know what action you want the user to take. How will you move them from a user to a prospect, to a warm lead, and ultimately to a client? Let's break this down.

- Target audience: Identify your clearly detailed persona.
- Clear call to action: Define the action you want the person to take.
- Media placement: Map out where your advertising will have the highest likelihood of connecting with your target audience, your persona. Don't be afraid to diversify your marketing mix by leveraging traditional and new media to get in front of your target audience.
- Creative: Decide what your ads will look like; images and words matter a great deal.
- Lead funnel: Know how leads will be managed as soon as they are generated.
- SEO: Continuously keep your website optimized for search engine keywords as well as conversational phrases.
- Search engine marketing: Leverage paid search to appear when people are actively looking for your services.
- Artificial intelligence: Understand how big data impact the power of your analytics as well as how artificial intelligence is evolving based on consumer behaviors.
- Social media marketing: Be authentic and social, offer expertise, provide free value, and link to your website.
- Analytics: Monitor and use your data; make adjustments to improve results.

Executing on a thoughtful digital strategy is absolutely a marathon, not a sprint. There are a lot of moving parts to a comprehensive and strategic digital strategy. Getting all of the pieces built and in place is the beginning phase, but then your digital strategy will evolve with you and your business. It will never be "done"; instead, it will ebb and flow. You may run the course of a set campaign, but even within the course of a campaign you can make tweaks and adjustments to optimize performance.

As your strategy begins to take shape, you can put a number of tactics in place to help you execute on your strategy. The layers of tactics implemented in a digital strategy create multiple opportunities to reach, connect with, and convert Charlotte and other identified personas. As you optimize campaigns in the digital space, you'll see conversions result in face-to-face meetings.

During the research and design stage, into execution, and continuing into tracking results of your campaigns, make Google your best friend. I am constantly telling our 5-year-old, who has a new best friend every day, that she can be friends with everyone. Be kind, be inviting, and make lots of friends. Fast forward to the adult digital marketing world and I will say the same thing about search engines and online directories: Play nice and engage with everyone . . . but in this case, make Google your very best friend. Here is a short list of Google activities to put on your own to-do list very early on:

- Establish a Gmail account for the business (yourbusinessname@gmail.com), then use this account for all of your business activity on Google. Whenever possible, do not mingle your personal accounts with the business account.
- Set up or gain access to your Google Analytics account. Spend time in there and get familiar with your website analytics. Work with your web developer if necessary; use them as a resource.
- Claim your Google My Business listing. Add details and photos and link this business listing to your website. When you add a blog post to social media, add a post to your business listing as well.

- Claim your location on Google Maps. Confirm or correct the address and contact information.
- Conduct similar setups by claiming the business listing on other directories, such as Bing, Yelp, Yahoo, and Yext.

Goal. Build Google competence into your annual goal setting. For example: By year-end I will be confident and comfortable navigating through the primary categories of Google Analytics, and I will understand what the data mean and how to use the data to influence our digital strategy.

Your #1 Digital Asset

Gone are the days of having no choice but to put your website in the hands of a website developer and then have any changes determined by their availability and fees. Don't get me wrong—I love website developers. When you really dig in and shape your website into a phenomenal tool for your business, it is incredibly helpful to have a go-to developer for support along your journey. *Support* is the key word. Find that trusted resource and build a strong relationship. Trust me when I say that website developers appreciate clients who put time and resources into their websites. They are there when you need them, there for big projects, there for troubleshooting, there for brainstorming and strategy sessions, and you are right there with them, working on this incredibly valuable digital asset. The time invested in learning how to manage your own website will provide return for the rest of your career.

The platform on which your site is built is called the content management system (CMS). The only way to learn how to use a CMS is to jump in and use it. Watch tutorials, take a local training course, play around and experiment, and click into sections you are not yet familiar with.

A great way to learn is to build your own personal website. Or, you can learn a huge amount working within the business website, whether you are on the live website, in private mode, or in a staging area. Either way, gain direction and a bit of guidance from your website developer and just jump in. Don't be afraid. Lean on your website developer to help you reach a nice comfort level so that you have no hesitation logging into your CMS and getting to work. When new software is thrust upon you, you learn how to use it, right? So tap into that space, even if it's a bit unfamiliar and challenging. Push yourself to tackle new software, knowing that the skills you will gain will have a tremendous impact on your ability to influence business growth and your own development and goals. As you dive deeper into your website, you will absolutely spend more and more time studying and interpreting the site analytics. Here is a short list of high-level analytics and why the data influence strategy. Remember, this is a short list; you will find so much useful information in your site analytics.

- New versus returning users
- Device and technology
- Bounce rate (the percentage of people who land on your site and exit without taking any additional action)
- Site content

This list is very basic and only scratches the surface. As your marketing and advertising become more strategic, watch the volume fluctuations in new versus returning users to your website. How a user intends to use a website varies greatly. Some users may be existing clients who are visiting to use an online bill-pay feature; others are prospects who are visiting to learn more as they consider a purchase. Or, they may be well outside your market and not at all likely to convert into a client, but they made their way to your website where they find useful information. The art of creating great user experiences (UXs) comes to fruition when data help guide design.

A while back at a seminar I heard someone say, "Design for mobile first and work backwards." That advice resonated loud and clear. After all, over the course of the past decade mobile traffic has rapidly exceeded desktop traffic for many industries. People are attached to their handheld devices, and this fact is a huge driver of user behavior. Google now rewards sites that are mobile friendly and use a responsive design, because they know that will provide their users with a great experience. So absolutely make sure your website is mobile-friendly. A responsive site design is coded to automatically adapt its design to display a certain way based on device dimensions (whether the device is a desktop, laptop, smartphone, etc.). Luckily for us marketers, CMSs have this valuable coding built right into the themes on their platform. All of that said, understanding the breakdown of mobile traffic versus desktop traffic to your website is important. In professional services marketing, many businesses' websites still receive the majority of site traffic during working hours, Monday through Friday, and the number of users visiting on desktop computers remains high. Watch and consider this metric; it helps inform strategy and UX design.

UX and load speed are both incredibly important. People don't like to wait for a site to load in a browser, and they want to have a great visual and navigation experience when they arrive. So what happens when these important things are not happening? The user will bounce right out of your website. These users constitute the bounce rate of a website. Perhaps your UX and load speed are both awesome but they just arrived on a site they have no interest in or need for. Either way, remember that a low bounce rate is good; it means most users are arriving to your website and staying beyond the first few seconds. A bounce rate does not mean that people are bouncing around to multiple pages of your website. Good bounce rates typically rest in the 35% to 50% range. If you run a digital ad campaign and 90%-plus bounce as soon as they arrive, you can use that data to identify ads and web pages that need to be adjusted. Just remember, a lower bounce rate is what you're shooting for.

Understanding how people navigate through your website will help you improve navigation and design; sometimes it will even influence which pages you choose to have users land on when entering your site. By studying which pages are the most frequently visited and where people go next, you can also identify pages where people tend to always exit your site.

Positive and negative indicators are all useful in UX design. A business owner or web developer outside the business may have great ideas for the website; just be sure that the data on how your visitors enter and interact with your website have a voice in the direction of this valuable asset as well. You are in a position to understand that data and provide that voice.

> **Goal.** Over the next six months, spend time with your website developer to build working knowledge of your CMS and identify areas for improvement.

Digital Network

All of the people you meet and all of the people you connect with should become part of your digital network. When you meet someone face-to-face, ask if you may add them to your email list. Tell them what sorts of things you send out and be sure to convey the value. Send follow-up messages and personally connect on LinkedIn.

What are you putting out there of value that exhibits your expertise and provides value to your target market? Is it a whitepaper, a monthly e-newsletter with useful articles, a how-to guide, a toolkit, or an industry trend report of 100 peer surveys? What do you have that you can use as a hook? Sending an e-newsletter is a good way to stay in front of your audience, clients included, and a very useful way to identify which topics are of the highest interest to your readers. Use the insights mined from your e-newsletter and frequently visited pages and posts to influence topics within your digital content.

When you determine what presents enough value for someone in your target audience to trade their email address for your free resource, you've helped them self-identify as a great prospect. When they receive your free download tool (e.g., whitepaper, industry report, template, guide), you've added a great prospect to your pipeline.

The best method to get that offer for a free tool and opportunity for email signup in front of people is to always drive your inbound traffic to the same landing page. If you're running pay-per-click ads, send them to your list-building landing page. If you're running Facebook ads, do the same. If you're linking to content on your blog, send them first to a squeeze page where maybe you've added a simple "Before we head to the article, we thought you would love our free guide, *10 Steps to Setting Up an LLC*," for example. Creating a squeeze page and directing inbound traffic there takes work and taps into your expertise but once you've created it, you can add it to your quiver of evergreen content. *Evergreen* means that it has staying power. You'll be able to use that content for a good long time.

Once someone has joined your email list, they've become a cherished and valued member of your audience. Use your email messages to build a relationship, letting them get to know you and how you communicate. With autoresponders you can craft messages and set them to send at specific intervals. Most email marketing platforms offer this capability. Here's how it works: When someone initially joins your list, you've got a welcome message ready to go and it hits their inbox instantly. Then a couple days later they receive another message; perhaps there you offer a link to a second giveaway or a useful LinkedIn article you've written along with an invitation to connect on LinkedIn or join your LinkedIn or Facebook group. A week later you send a check-in email to ask how they liked the initial free resource and include a case study that illustrates how the same practices worked in a specific situation. And now you're running a drip marketing campaign!

Watch your email analytics and set up triggers in your email system—there are many to choose from—to send specific emails when your user takes a specific action. For example, say they opened your follow-up message and downloaded the second giveaway. Lead them down a path of your own design. That second download identified them as a very engaged and very receptive member of your audience. For those who are actively consuming and engaging with your content—in other words, getting to know, like, and trust you—tee them up for a more personal experience. Help them enter the conversion phase of your lead funnel.

Invite them to sign up for a live webinar, to view a prerecorded video series, or to attend an event at which you'll be speaking, or offer a one-to-one phone consult. Determine what works well for you and your market. Are you corresponding with people locally, regionally, nationally, or globally? When you're moving from the relationship-building phase to the conversion phase, you've got to take an approach that works for you. To figure out what works, try a few things. Once you begin to get results from the most successful conversion method, you can home in on that and refine it even further.

We just walked through a high-level crash course in robust email marketing tactics. Take a breath—don't get overwhelmed! This level of sophistication takes time and much trial and error. But when you're ready, you can absolutely do this! Go put your audience at the center of your thought process. Ask yourself (and your data) how your audience consumes content.

Rookie Tip #1: Don't just set it and forget it. The beauty of digital marketing is that you have oodles of data right at your fingertips. When you use these data to make improvements and changes as you go, your ROI will improve. Alternatively, if you set up a digital campaign and just let it sit out there or you have a website that you never touch, your results will suffer. You wouldn't book a performance hall and design a set without also casting the actors and selling tickets, would you?

Rookie Tip #2: Build your network. Always be adding connections to your network. Consider peers, colleagues, prospects, fellow club or organization members, new acquaintances, and thought leaders. If you met face-to-face, follow up with a LinkedIn connection request and a personalized message. When you build relationships and contact information is mounting in an email account, be sure that you keep a personal file of your key industry contacts, including people in the local media, vendors, mentors, and go-to peer resources. You spend a great deal of time building relationships, so stay organized when it comes to people's contact information. As people move along through their career, stay connected on LinkedIn.

Goal. Become an active user on LinkedIn. Over the course of the next three months, create a routine for building time on LinkedIn into your weekly schedule. In that three-month period, complete multiple sections of your profile, ensure experiences are linked to appropriate business pages, and ask a few close colleagues and acquaintances for recommendations. Solidify a routine for adding people to your network.

7

Getting Creative

Not everyone in marketing chooses this path because they love the collision of creativity with business, of psychology with analytics. But some do, and I posit that many who choose a career path in marketing develop a deep appreciation for all of these facets of the profession. If you've truly found your professional calling, I suspect you might even love the collision of creative and analytics!

You may be like me and have a knack for the arts. I love it all. Whether drawing, painting, design, photography, or mixed media, you name it, I enjoy creating it, soaking it in, escaping to the artist's plane. But you know what? Life is so crazy hectic that there are spells of very little to no fine arts in the day-to-day, but boy is there plenty of creativity. When you bring this awareness and perspective into a business, you bring a unique vantage point and skill set. Don't ever undervalue or underestimate the unique perspective you bring to the table or the positive impact you can have on a business. In a world where people need innovative thinkers and variety of thought, your voice has never been more valuable and sought after. Embrace that and show up to the table with preparedness and purpose.

But what if you're not like that? What if you're telling yourself that isn't you, that you are not creative and never have been? To that I say, "Stop!" Enough time has been spent walking down the road of negative self-fulfilling prophecies. It's time to turn that sentiment on its head and recognize that we are all creative. Are we all masters of media, capable of works destined for the National Gallery? Of course not. But we are capable of studying and observing creative concepts that grab us and pull us in. We are all capable of telling ourselves, "I am creative." We are all intricate and diverse beings. At our unique and individual core, we are all members of creation. However you slice and dice it, you do have it in you to embrace and foster your creativity. We all do.

Now that we're all smocked up and ready to roll, let's enter into the world of the marketing generalist. Creativity rests firmly in advertising, graphic design, website development, branding, interior and experiential design, media production, and copywriting. As you can see, this is a highly charged right-brained profession.

But make no mistake about it—you won't be letting the analytical left side of your brain go dormant. Quite the contrary. When you approach business problem solving, financial analysis, process improvement, market analysis, data analysis, team dynamics, interpersonal relationships—all of the intricate and interrelated parts that make up a business—with a creative and open mind, your input will be broad in nature and valuable beyond measure. Developing your skills as a marketer will develop your skills as a critical thinker and creative problem solver.

Logo File Portfolio

Have you ever worked with a vendor on a project and been told that you sent the logo file in the wrong format? We touched on this in the "Get Your Assets in Order" chapter. There are so many things to learn about graphic design that will make you a stronger marketing generalist. Just remember that, like anything, it takes time to develop new skills. Even knowing the different file types and what to give vendors when they ask is an enormously helpful foundation. So let's walk through what file types you need and the circumstances in which you'll use them.

JPG. When you import images from a camera or take an image with your phone, the file type created is a JPG (which is short for "Joint Photographic Experts Group," who created it). Think of a JPG as a picture file of your logo. There will always be a background in the file, just as there is always a background in a picture. When you print a JPG file, it will maintain clarity as long as the image is not manipulated or scaled larger than its original size. A JPG is appropriate for Web or print use.

GIF. GIF, which stands for "graphics interchange format," has made a surge in recent years with the addition of recommended GIFs for inclusion in texts and social posts. A GIF file may be a few images strung together to create a movement and animation or graphic elements set to timings and transitions to create movement. These are most appropriate for Web use.

PNG. PNG, which stands for "portable network graphics," is used on the Web and in print applications where a transparent background is necessary. When you see a logo plunked onto a colored background and the logo rests on its very own block of background color, you know it was not a PNG file. If it were, the logo would rest on the background color of the file itself. The reverse is also true: You may get a black background surrounding your logo when you place a PNG file on a white Web background. PNG files are appropriate for Web and print use.

PDF. PDF, which is short for "portable document format," preserves the integrity of text, images, and layout within a file. You've likely used PDF files many times. Graphic design vendors request this format to acquire a vector-based file of your logo. PDF files are appropriate for print and digital viewing as a stand-alone PDF file.

AI or EPS. AI stands for "Adobe Illustrator," and EPS stands for "encapsulated PostScript." These formats preserve the integrity of images for high-quality printing. Adobe Illustrator or other Adobe

Creative Suite applications are used to create the source file, also called the original working file. Within these applications you have the ability to save as EPS. If you are asked for a vector-based file, one of these formats will do the trick.

One step in particular will be well worth the time and effort: stock up your logo file folder. Not many people have an animated logo file, but all the other formats listed here are great to have prepped and on hand when you need them, and you'll need them quite a bit. If you do not have a vector-formatted logo, the process you'll go through to create one and then to create the additional formats is a valuable one. If you're just learning new software, creating your logo is great practice, because logos are typically on the simpler side, with only a few elements. You can do this! If you get stuck, find some software how-to videos to quickly guide you through the steps you are still learning. I'll say it again: You can do this!

While you're in logo creation mode, you can also create two additional formats that will be needed over time: a white version of your logo, which is typically used with a transparent background, and a brand mark, which is created by isolating any icon or emblem in your logo and saving it as a separate file. A brand mark is incredibly powerful when used as your profile image for social media business pages. Be sure to check out the marketing resources page at hillarydow.com for a super-useful guide of image dimensions for social profiles.

Once your logo assets are in order, you'll have a folder of graphics and logos you can easily and quickly get to, and boom—all of these formats will be right at your fingertips whenever you need them. Doesn't that sound awesome? Doesn't that sound like a project that will make your life easier and help promote the business in a more polished and professional manner? Say goodbye to fuzzy, logo graphics that are too small, and say hello to getting it done well! I'll tell you what, vendors who create branded promotional items and advertising partners will absolutely love and appreciate this effort. Your dedication and work behind this effort will pay dividends for years to come.

What if you're just learning the basics of Illustrator and you know that having a complete AI file is a long way off from completion? Keep learning. Don't get discouraged; know that many wonderful resources are available to help you along the way.

Working With Agencies and Freelancers

Wherever you land on the creative learning curve, don't forget that freelance graphic designers and agencies are ready to help you. The first time I worked with an agency, a small local boutique agency, was during the beginning stages of designing a new logo for the company where I worked. I'd designed several logo concepts, but there was nothing that I absolutely fell in love with. After going through the concepts with the firm's managing partner, he too lacked a wow moment or pull to any one of my designs. It was in that meeting that I got feedback that was exactly what I needed to hear: "Hillary, it's OK to ask for help. You have a lot of talents, but there will always be things you need to get done that aren't your strongest skill set. Don't get stuck or discouraged. Just seek out a little help." Did I continue to practice and hone my own graphic design skills? Absolutely. But I also recognized that my mentor was giving me honest advice and support, and it led me to develop an entirely new set of skills as a marketing generalist: learning how to work with and maximize the contributions of creative freelancers and advertising agencies.

Think of yourself as a general contractor. Not many people can build a house by themselves, right? You've got a solid and ever-developing skill set. One skill in particular is knowing how to surround yourself with, and lean on, the "electrician" (website developer), the "painting crew" (graphic designers), the "heating & cooling specialist" (copywriter), the "plumber" (digital marketing specialist), and so on. Being aware of skill gaps and the power of leveraging resources to achieve great things is a powerful skill unto itself for a marketing generalist. You are just like the contractor who couldn't possibly complete a project without subcontractors. Surround yourself with tested and trusted resources.

Where do you find those resources? Tap your local community for talent, use online freelance pools, connect with resources at training and events, research full-service and niche agencies, and always, always, always do your research. Understand who they are, how they work, and what services they provide. Review examples of previous work and their reporting format (and drill down on those examples), and be sure to fully understand how they structure fees and contracts. You could have project-based work or an ongoing engagement structured more like a monthly retainer. With boutique and local agencies, you may have an enhanced connection because you see their staff when you run around town and you're all friends on Facebook. Or, you may wrap your investment around a niche agency located halfway across the continent that offers full-service support specializing in your specific industry or their specific tactic. Better yet, over time you can develop the skills of a rockstar marketing generalist, whereby you leverage skills and expertise from all types of outsourced talent. Because, let's be honest, a marketing generalist is often operating as a department of one. Your ability to effectively select and manage outsourced talent can be the difference between mediocre results and exceptional return on strategic investments.

Many websites now offer great user experiences when looking for and working with freelance service providers. Fiverr is a great example of a talent pool of individuals who can help you fill in skills gaps. A recent search for "logo vector file" yielded 6,156 experts, with search filters to help narrow down the results. I've worked with a lovely young lady, a college student studying graphic design, to generate a whiteboard video that was used during the launch of a systemwide human resource initiative. I had two main reasons for initiating the project with a freelance designer:

1. The project required technical skills to efficiently accomplish, and the team did not have the skillset or capacity to manage the project at that time.

2. Time was a precious and scarce resource, which rightly placed some items on the priority list and others on a "nice to have" but not imperative list. To provide best-in-class service to our internal clients and leadership across the healthcare system, we needed to accomplish tasks on both lists, so we leveraged outsourcing for expertise and efficiency.

Another personal example comes from creating a book cover design for this book. The goal was to put out the best book cover design possible, with the resources available. As with most design projects, I could have done it myself, but I preferred to put my time into writing and marketing, and I knew in my heart the design would be more polished when done by someone else, so I did my research. By reading about the experiences of other first-time publishers and watching tips and tricks generously shared on YouTube, I learned the ins and outs of the process used by 99designs.com. Like fiverr, this site has created a pool of graphic design freelancers who review your design brief and submit design concepts to enter your design contest. With different levels of investment, you have access to increasing numbers of concepts and increasingly skilled designers. I went all in. My financial investment was at the bronze level, and I made it a priority for 10 days to engage with the designers, invite those who didn't initially submit designs, and give very thoughtful feedback. Over the course of the contest I had just shy of 200 concepts and iterations of book covers as the designers worked through refining their work. The process was fun and exciting and resulted in a great book cover. You're reading this book now, so I ask you—How did I do?

Much work remains to be done that doesn't align quite as well as projects do with freelance outsourcing. When you're looking for marketing support in your local area, start with a few simple searches.

- Run some Google searches and study websites of local marketing agencies.
- Search Facebook pages for "marketing" and filter results for local business or place.
- Search your local Chamber of Commerce directories, so you can support fellow members.
- Search state chapters and organizations for marketing, public relations, and social media professionals.
- Ask for recommendations from people whose marketing you admire.
- Scout talent at seminars, events, and webinars and then research the person/agency.

Once you've gathered a short list of potential matches, reach out and schedule time to meet with someone to discuss your needs. It's amazing what you'll learn about capabilities and fit when you sit down and have a conversation with people. Listen for the types of questions they ask. How are they building an understanding of your business needs? Pay attention to your comfort level. Are you feeling at ease and engaged or like something is not quite connecting? The stronger the fit, the more successful the relationship will be.

Not quite sure what to ask during an introductory meeting? After all, you're both feeling out whether it makes sense to launch a working partnership. Here are some suggestions:

- What are the drivers that differentiate your sluggish client relationships from those that consistently make progress and achieve outstanding outcomes?
- How do you measure campaign results? May I see an example of how you report results back to clients?
- Will I work directly with you, an account manager, or multiple people?
- What is a reasonable expectation for turnaround times on work?
- How do you structure contracts?

As you work your way through the answers to these questions, also keep in mind how all of your interactions play out, including email correspondence, chit-chat, and rapport building, as well as punctuality, comfort level, and feelings of fit. The better the fit, the stronger your working relationship tends to be.

When you've sat in both the client and the freelance consultant seats, as I have, you gain a strong appreciation for the behaviors that drive the most successful outcomes. At the center of it all lies open and trusted communication paired with consistent and timely follow-through. Someone working from the outside looking in needs an internal partner who is committed and engaged in the process. If there is a lack of engagement, the work will slog along with the real potential of stalling completely. Without internal guidance and commitment, the freelancer or agency can't possibly have the information they need to make their work truly representational of the client.

You have a tremendous opportunity to knock this out of the park. When you remain present and engaged, your work in partnership with agencies and freelance consultants magnifies your ability to influence and move the needle on the growth potential, culture, and direction of your organization.

Whatever the task or objective before you, embrace your creative side. Silence the self-doubt and believe in the power of your personal contribution. There will always be a need for creative thinking and problem solving, visual representations of your brand, and an ability to stand out. Believe that you are exceptional, and your work will be too.

8

Living It

With all of the inspiration and resources that surround you, the universe of like-minded people is supportive and rallying for you to succeed. You'll find a community that suits you and provides ideas, inspiration, and answers, if you only go looking for it.

The right community can inspire you; it can provide tools and resources to build your skills and boost your confidence. It is up to *you* to turn ideas into action, plans into follow-through, and dreams into reality.

Early in my career I made my way to an after-hours event hosted by our local group for young professionals. The Young Professionals of the Lewiston-Auburn Area, YPLAA (pronounced "why play"), was a group organized under the umbrella of the local Chamber of Commerce. With digital communities still in the pre-Myspace days and certainly long before Facebook groups, we had only our own backyard to look to for community and support. We still do. At that point I found and built my community within YPLAA. Friends, peers, clients, colleagues, mentors, and fellow committee and board members—the list goes on, and my network blossomed. As a matter of fact, my book editor is a wonderful and talented woman I befriended through YPLAA.

I joined committees, served as YPLAA chair, and was later appointed to local boards for which I rose to the responsibility of board president. As my career developed, so too did my community involvement. Without a shadow of a doubt, I link the successful progression of my career to my civic engagement and commitment to helping others. I showed up, and I continue to show up. I also now belong to a global community of authors, digital CEOs, and leaders. Finding ways and places to surround yourself with like-minded people is an important part of the journey.

Everything begins with you. Ask yourself these questions:

- Are you committed to constantly learning new skills?
- Are you fully present in all areas of your life?
- Do you give of your time, talents, and resources to help others?
- Do you take care of yourself?
- Are you consistent in contributing your best work?
- Are you focused?
- Do you believe in yourself?

I can offer you words of encouragement and share wisdom I've gained over time. But it all boils down to you. What you set your mind to, and then choose to follow through with, is how your path will be defined. Do you remember the analogy of the tree whose bark has been smoothed over time, after repeatedly having had hands grasp it for support? While that tree can be helpful for a time, it is rooted in one spot. You're not.

You're nearly done reading this book, so you clearly have a desire to learn and develop new skills. You are moving forward. Keep that momentum going.

I shared the example of how YPLAA provided opportunity and a network of amazing people as I navigated the early stages of my marketing career. I was, and eventually Adam and I were both, out and about all the time. Early morning Chamber breakfasts, lunchtime networking groups, paddling events, costume parties, after-hours events, weekend fundraisers—you name it, we were there. Both social by nature, both in positions where networking fueled business relationships, we were doing it all and loving every minute of it. One day we were in the checkout line of a local department store and the cashier, having seen our candid photos in many "out and about" event recaps, said to us, "Oh my goodness, you're the Dows from *LA Magazine!*" No joke. We still get a chuckle out of it now and again.

But who are we? Just a couple of everyday working professionals doing what we love to do. We're fully committed to our work, our family, our own development, and our community. But this approach doesn't suit everyone, nor does it suit every stage of life. We were both in the public eye far more frequently before we had children, then our focus shifted and we scaled back on the events and after-hours commitments. Living our truth and having a life filled with meaning on all fronts is something we embraced. We still do.

The right mix and balance between work and personal energy lie in where you receive the greatest value, joy, and positive outcomes. Following the data to drive marketing activities is as important as following personal values and discipline to achieve great things in your life. The use of the words *mix* and *balance* is incredibly meaningful. There is rarely, if ever, true balance in life. The trick is finding the right mix of work, family, personal, community, and worldly experiences. This concoction called life presents glimpses of balance at times, but embracing the chaos that includes deep, meaningful experiences is a path laden with adventure, excitement, love, success, challenge, and all of the things that make for a life full of riches.

My hope for you is that you're discovering rewards along with the challenges that inevitably accompany the marketing department of one, the marketing generalist. I hope this book has served as a tool, a resource, and, above all, an inspiration. The path you're on is filled with opportunity and growth. As your journey continues, I'd like to remind you that yes, you can do this! You simply need to keep moving forward and tackle what lies ahead with an open mind and eager spirit.

Until our paths cross again, know that others believe in you and, most important, believe in yourself.

Truth: You wear many hats throughout your daily grind. Who doesn't in the fast-paced world of professional services? One thing is for sure: When focused on marketing, advertising, and networking, you feel like you've found your comfort zone. You simply love the collision of creativity, business, technology, and bringing people together. Ideas, action, and making true human connections motivate and inspire you. Do these statements describe you?

You may be a marketing rookie, but you know you have the potential to be a full-on, bona fide marketing rockstar! If you're ready to own it, to do the work and become the amazing marketing professional you know is in there, this book is for you. Tips, checklists, examples, rookie tips, goal-setting exercises—seriously, get ready to learn and be psyched!

I get it. I've been there. I'd love nothing more than to help and inspire you along your journey. Let's get started!

www.ingramcontent.com/pod-product-compliance
Lightning Source LLC
Chambersburg PA
CBHW070942210326
41520CB00021B/7020